PSYCHIATRIC CASE
CLERKING FOR
MEDICAL STUDENTS

....

SHARMILLA KANAGASUNDRAM

To order additional copies of this book, contact
Toll Free +65 3165 7531 (Singapore)
Toll Free +60 3 3099 4412 (Malaysia)
www.partridgepublishing.com/singapore
orders.singapore@partridgepublishing.com

ISBN
978-1-5437-4965-6 (sc)
978-1-5437-4966-3 (e)

Print information available on the last page.

08/29/2022

PARTRIDGE

PROLOGUE

This book PSYCHIATRIC CASE CLERKING FOR MEDICAL STUDENTS has its origins during the pandemic (2020-2022) when the biweekly tutorials for the medical students were held through zoom, google meet and teams. Wondering if students could understand what was being said I decided to make a word document which I sent to the tutorial students. Then I realized that this document actually simplified my work and produced better results in terms of completeness of clerking. In addition, I felt that this compilation made clerking simple, systematic and easy to understand for the undergraduate medical students. The contents of this book has previously been applied during my tutorials on many batches of medical students for over 18 years with good results.

This book should not be used alone but in conjunction with both the Malaysian Clinical Practice Guidelines for schizophrenia, bipolar disorder and major depressive disorder with regards to treatment of the afore mentioned disorders as well as a recommended psychiatric text book. This book focuses more on clinical aspects of schizophrenia, bipolar disorder and major depressive disorder.

ACKNOWLEDGEMENT

I would like to acknowledge University Malaya for giving me the opportunity to work here. It has been a great learning experience for me.

CONTENTS

SECTION 1

HISTORY TAKING AND MENTAL STATE EXAMINATION

1. Chief Complaint and Duration

Use the own words of the patient, relative or informant.

An example of a chief complaint would be: Hearing sounds or voices when alone for two days. Don't use technical terms: such as "The patient complained of hallucinations". Hallucination being the medical term. This is because the patient does not know what exactly constitutes a hallucination.

2. History of Present Illness

Use the patient's own words.

For example: Don't say "hallucination". Instead say that the patient can hears things that other people cannot hear.

1. Start THE HISTORY OF PRESENT ILLNESS from when the patient was last well. For a case of schizophrenia you need to ascertain the baseline and consider that to be a period of wellness. If the patient is currently 33 years of age and has been having schizophrenia since he was 20 years old, then HISTORY OF PRESENT ILLNESS WILL start from this recent episode and not 20 years of age.
2. CHRONOLOGICAL ORDER: Write symptoms in the order how they appeared with the duration e. g poor sleep for the last three weeks, then low mood for the last two weeks.
3. Each of the symptoms must have the duration as well.
    E.g. Feeling like some one is following him the last two weeks.

State the relevant positives and the relevant negatives for

1. Organicity (headache, salivation, fits, up-rolled eyeballs, confusion, Generalized tonic clonic, blurred vision, disorientation to time, place and person)
2. Depressive episode.
3. Manic episode.
4. Psychosis (Delusions, hallucinations, first rank symptoms)
5. Anxiety (Generalized anxiety disorder and panic attacks)

State the psychosocial stressors

1. Explore the possible stressors such as marriage/ relationships/school/college/ work/bullying/finances/in laws.
2. The stressor must precipitate or cause or exacerbate the symptoms. Some time there are a few stressors that cause SNOWBALLING.

State the level of functioning after falling ill during the history of present illness.

i. Is the patient still able to go to work or study?
ii. Is the patient still able to carry out the activities of daily living (ADL)?

3. Past Medical History

The objective of the past medical history is to:-

1)Restart the previous medication that the patient has been taking for other concomitant medical conditions in case the patient is admitted to the ward.

2)Psychiatric medication may increase chances of developing metabolic syndrome so we have to know if the patient already has metabolic syndrome.

3) Inquire for history of

- Diabetes mellitus as it can predispose to low mood. Metformin the drug that is used to treat diabetes can also cause low mood.
- Hypertension
- Ischaemic heart disease
- Fits or epilepsy can cause post ictal psychosis or depression.
- Bronchial asthma with steroid use.
  Steroids can cause psychosis and low mood.
- Hyperthyroidism or hypothyroidism
- Parkinsons disease can cause psychosis, depression or dementia
- Systemic Lupus Erythematosus- can be associated with get psychosis, cognitive problem, depressions. The high dose of prednisolone that is given in SLE can cause psychological symptoms.

4. Past Surgical History

Any history of operation so that we can elicit if the patient has other medical comorbidities.

5. Past Psychiatric History

Ascertain the age of onset of psychiatric illness, symptoms, stressors, response to medication, Ascertain the longest period the patient was well and level of functioning. This is important to ascertain factors that may maintain the patient in wellness. How many admissions to the psychiatric ward in the past. This will give an idea to the severity of the illness. The number of previous admissions may indicate non -compliance or non- adherence to medication, poor response to medication, on going problems, poor coping, poor support or poor insight. Ascertain if there are any side effects to the medications. Any previous history of depot injections or electro convulsive therapy.

INTEREPISODE: How well is the patient in between episodes? What is the best level of functioning after the patient fell ill?

6. Substance History

With respect to substances it is necessary to find out why the patient began to take the substance. Was the substance use to self -medicate his/her anxiety or low mood or was it due to peer pressure. It is necessary to find out whom the patient takes the substance with, the duration and the quantity used. It is necessary to find out where the patient got the money to buy these substances. Has the patient ever tried to detox from the use and if so how long was he or she free from it. Did the patient ever get into trouble with the law for using it and how the use has impacted the patient's life and his or her role in family function.

A. HEROIN

> Heroin use can be intravenous or by chasing. If it is intravenous do inquire for infections such as hepatitis B and HIV.

B. AMPHETAMINE

> Amphetamine use is by pills, powder, crystals and liquids.

C. CANNABIS

> Cannabis can be smoked or eaten.

D. ALCOHOL

> Do find out the number of units used. Ascertain the presence of associated complications such as gastritis, memory impairments, loss of libido and past head injuries.

E. NICOTINE

> How many cigarettes smoked daily?

7. Premorbid Personality

- How does the patient cope with stress?

- What is the patient's predominant mood—generally happy, pessimistic, depressed or anxious?
- How does the patient spend her or his free time?
- Does the patient have many friends?
- Does she think people like her or him?

8. Family History

Find out if any family members had mental illness, what were their symptoms, are they on treatment and any admissions for mental illness,

Find out who are the members of the family, their ages, occupation and if parents have remarried. Elaborate on relationship between siblings and step siblings if present.

GENEOLOGY CHART

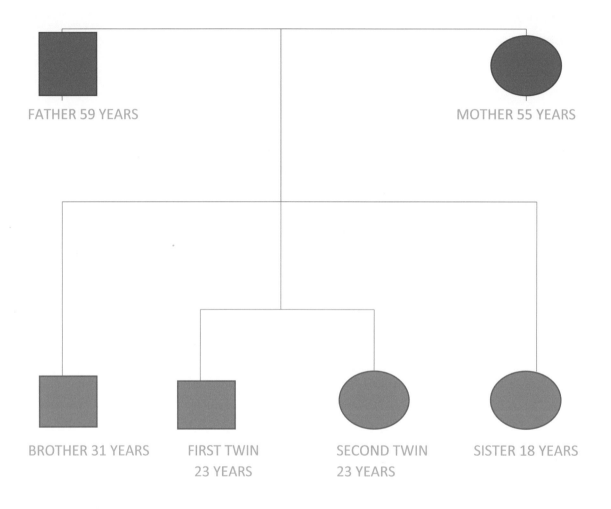

FATHER 59 YEARS

MOTHER 55 YEARS

BROTHER 31 YEARS

FIRST TWIN
23 YEARS

SECOND TWIN
23 YEARS

SISTER 18 YEARS

9. Personal History—

State the place the patient was born.
<u>Education</u>

State the schools, colleges and institutes of higher education that the patient attended.

State the grades. A decline in results can signify onset in illness.

Involvement in extracurricular activities can show premorbid personality.
<u>Job history</u>

Start with the first job the patient held.
The nature of the job and the description of what the patient was supposed to do.
What was the longest period the job was held?
Find out if the patient had ever been promoted. This can signify good level of function.
Find out if the patient has ever been fired from any job. If so the reason.
Find out the sexual orientation of the patient.

10. <u>Mental State Examination</u>

1. **APPEARANCE**: For example :-
   A well- groomed young Chinese lady dressed in a skirt and blouse.
   Look for extra pyramidal symptoms, presence of tremors or poor eye contact.
   Mention if there are any tattoos, make up or jewellery.
   Scars on head may suggest fainting episodes and possible history of fits.
   Scars on the inner aspect of wrist and thigh may suggest self- harm
   Cigarette burns may suggest abuse or self- harm behaviors.
   Presence of tremors.

2. **BEHAVIOUR**—fidgetiness, presence of stereotypy, presence of mannerisms
3. **STATE WHETHER THE PATIENT IS COOPERATIVE TO BE EXAMINED OR NOT**
4. **SPEECH**—relevant/rational/coherent
5. **MOOD**—angry/sad/depressed/anxious/happy
6. **AFFECT** can be described in 3 ways
   - Appropriate to the mood (The patient says he is feeling sad and looks sad as well. This is seen in cases of depression)

Inappropriate to the mood (patient says he is feeling sad but is smiling or laughing. This may be seen in some cases of schizophrenia)
- happy, sad, anxious, depressed
- normal, restricted, blunted, flat. (Presents as a continuum with normal and flat being the extremes.)

7. **PERCEPTUAL DISTURBANCES**
Check for the presence of various types of hallucinations (auditory, visual, olfactory, tactile, gustatory,)

8. **COGNITION**
Cognition has many components.

MEMORY

- **LONG TERM MEMORY**---Ask for date of birth
- **RECENT MEMORY**---Ask what the patient ate for breakfast.
- **IMMEDIATE REGISTRATION**—Name 5 objects not in the room then ask the patient to repeat what you said. This is impaired in dementia.
- **5 MINUTE RECALL**—After 5 minutes the patient should remember and tell you the same 5 objects. This is impaired in dementia

ATTENTION AND CONCENTRATION

- **SERIAL 7**
The patient needs to subtract 7 from 100 until he reaches 2.
- **DIGIT SPAN**
The examiner needs to say 5 numbers to the patient. The numbers should not be consecutive. For example 6,9,3,4,1.
The patient needs to be able to repeat the 5 numbers forward (6,9,3,4,1) and 4 backward (4,3,9,6).
- **SPELL WORLD BACKWARDS**
(DLROW)

ORIENTATION

- **TIME**---time of day/date / day/ month / year
  SHOULD BE INTACT IN SCHIZOPHRENIA AND BIPOLAR. IF THE PATIENT CANNOT TELL IT IS MORNING OR NIGHT OR DOES NOT KNOW THE TIME OF DAY, CONSIDER DELIRIUM
- **PLACE**---the ward, name of hospital, which floor, country, city
- **PERSON**---must be able to recognize the family

ABSTRACTION

- **PROVERB TEST**
  For example
  Meaning of "kaki ayam"," kaki botol"," a stitch in time saves nine", "a bird in hand is better than two in a bush".
- **ASK SIMILARITIES BETWEEN 2 DIFFERENT OBJECTS**
  For example:--
  1)Similarities between apple and orange
  2)Similarities between bus and car
  3)Similarities between ruler and pencil

INSIGHT—Describe Insight as either GOOD, FAIR or POOR. The student must ask

- if the patient knows he has a mental illness
- if he or she thinks that they need medication
- if he or she thinks his or her experiences are real
- if he or she thinks that others think their experiences are real.

Antipsychotics can and generally improves a patient's insight. However, this improvement may not be seen in every patient. Hence psychosis improves independently of insight. Poor insight is found in as many as 90% of schizophrenic patients.

SECTION 2

DIFFERENTIAL DIAGNOSES FOR PSYCHOTIC, MANIC AND DEPRESSIVE EPISODES

DIFFERENTIAL DIAGNOSIS

This section of the book aims to make it easy for the student to come up with differential diagnoses based on the psychological symptoms elicited in the HOPI.

IF THE PATIENT PRESENTS WITH PSYCHOSIS THEN CONSIDER THE FOLLOWING DIAGNOSES

1. **ORGANICITY**
   - SECONDARY TO GENERAL MEDICAL CONDITION –DELIRIUM, HYPERTHYROIDISM, BRAIN TUMOR, POST ICTAL CONFUSION, SLE, PARKINSON DISEASE AND WILSON DISEASE.
   - SECONDARY TO SUBSTANCE USE----CANNABIS, AMPHETAMINES
2. **BRIEF PSYCHOTIC DISORDER (<30 DAYS)**
3. **SCHIZOPHRENIFORM DISORDER (MORE THAN 1 MONTH <6 MONTHS)**
4. **SCHIZOPHRENIA (MORE THAN 6 MONTHS)**

IF THE PATIENT PRESENTS WITH A MANIC EPISODE THEN CONSIDER THE FOLLOWING DIAGNOSES

1. **ORGANICITY**
   - SECONDARY TO GENERAL MEDICAL CONDITION –HYPERTHYROIDISM, RIGHT SIDED BRAIN TUMOR, SLE,
   - SECONDARY TO SUBSTANCE USE—AMPHETAMINES
2. **BIPOLAR DISORDER IN MANIC PHASE**
3. **SCHIZOAFFECTIVE DISORDER BIPOLAR SUBTYPE**

IF THE PATIENT PRESENTS WITH A DEPRESSIVE EPISODE THEN CONSIDER THE FOLLOWING DIAGNOSES

1) **ORGANICITY—**
   - SECONDARY TO GENERAL MEDICAL CONDITION –HYPOTHYROIDISM, LEFT SIDED BRAIN TUMOR, PARKINSON DISEASE, SLE, DIABETES MELLITUS, EPILEPSY, ANEMIA
   - SUBSTANCE USE—WITHDRAWAL OF ALCOHOL, WITHDRAWAL OF AMPHETAMINES, WITHDRAWAL OF HEROIN
2) **MAJOR DEPRESSIVE DISORDER**
3) **BIPOLAR DISORDER IN DEPRESSED PHASE**
4) **PERSISTENT DEPRESSIVE DISORDER**
5) **ADJUSTMENT DISORDER**
6) **SCHIZOAFFECTIVE DISORDER DEPRESSED TYPE**
7) **NORMAL SADNESS**

SECTION 3

GENERAL OVERVIEW OF MANAGEMENT

<u>MANAGEMENT OF COMMON PSYCHIATRIC CASES</u>

Management of all cases is divided into **investigations** and **treatment**:-

BIOPSYCHOSOCIAL INVESTIGATION
- **MANAGEMENT DEPENDS ON THE INDIVIDUAL PATIENT OR IS INDIVIDUALISED TO A PARTICULAR PATIENT.**

BIOPSYCHOSOCIAL TREATMENT
- **TREATMENT MAY NOT INCLUDE ALL THE BELOW AT ONCE.**
- **TREATMENT IS SELECTED ON A CASE BY CASE BASIS.**

MALAYSIAN CPG—CLINICAL PRACTICE GUIDELINES. PLEASE DOWNLOAD FROM THE INTERNET

GENERAL OVERVIEW OF MANAGEMENT

	BIOLOGICAL	PSYCHOLOGICAL	SOCIAL
INVESTIGATION	• FULL BLOOD COUNT • FASTING BLOOD SUGAR • RENAL FUNCTION • LIVER FUNCTION • SERUM T4/TSH • CTSCAN BRAIN • ECG **IF INFECTION IS SUSPECTED** 1. EEG **IF DEMENTIA IS SUSPECTED** 1. SERUM FOLATE/B12 2. SERUM CA/MG PHOSPHATE	QUESTIONNAIRES/ RATING SCALES	HISTORY TAKING

	BIOLOGICAL	PSYCHOLOGICAL	SOCIAL
TREATMENT	• THERAPEUTIC DRUGS • ELECTROCONVULSIVE THERAPY **PLEASE USE THE MALAYSIAN CLINICAL PRACTICE GUIDELINES FOR THE EXACT BIOLOGICAL TREATMENTS REQUIRED FOR THE SPECIFIC DISORDERS.**	• PSYCHOEDUCATION • SUPPORTIVE PSYCHOTHREAPY • COGNITIVE BEHAVIOUR THERAPY • COUPLE THERAPY • FAMILY THERAPY • PSYCHODYNAMIC THERAPY • ANGER MANAGEMENT • RELAXATION THERAPY • SOCIAL SKILLS • DIALECTICAL BEHAVIOUR THERAPY FOR BORDERLINE PERSONALITY DISORDER	ENVIRONMENTAL MODIFICATION

SECTION 4

HELPFUL QUESTIONS TO ELICIT SYMPTOMS

Questions to ask to elicit symptoms of a depressive episode

PLEASE MAKE SURE THAT THE ASSOCIATED SYMPTOMS OCCUR IN THE SAME TIME PERIOD AS THE LOW MOOD

1. **Mood**
   May I know how has your mood been over the last 2 weeks?
   Is the mood the same throughout the day or is it worse in the morning?
   This is to look for diurnal variation in the mood
   When happy things happen does your mood get better?
   This is to look for reactivity in the mood
   The mood is less sad when there is reactivity.

2. **Anhedonia**
   Do you have interest in activities that previously made you happy?
   How did you spend your free time in the past?
   Do you have to force yourself to work?
   Do you enjoy your work?

3. **Sleep**
   Find out what are the normal timings of going to bed and waking up.
   How is it different during the episode of low mood?
   Look for initial, terminal and middle insomnia.
   Initial Insomnia==Problem to fall asleep
   Middle insomnia—multiple awakenings
   Terminal insomnia—awakening at least 2 hours before the normal awakening time

4. **Appetite and weight change**
   How is your appetite now compared to when your mood was normal?
   Any weight gain or loss during the period of low mood?
   Are your clothes more loose/ tighter now?

5. **How is your concentration?**

6. **Do you feel guilty about anything?**

7. **Hopelessness**
   How do you see your future?
   Do you feel you can solve your problems (stressor)?
   If you cannot solve your problems what will you do?
   Can you accept the problem as it is?
   That means if the problem cannot be solved can you accept it?

8. **Worthlessness**
   Any feelings that you are not a useful person?

9. **Suicidal thoughts (The presence of suicidal thoughts must be looked for in every patient)**

   Have you ever thought that it is better not to be alive?
   Have you ever contemplated taking your life?
   Were the suicidal thoughts fleeting (lasts for a few seconds only) or persistent (think about suicide for hours)?
   When was that you had suicidal thoughts?
   Any previous attempt at suicide?
   Do you have a plan how you want to commit suicide?
   What did you do when you had such thoughts?
   What has stopped (prevented) you from committing suicide? (THE THOUGHT THAT STOPS THE PERSON IS THE PROTECTIVE FACTOR. NORMALLY PATIENT HAS CHILDREN OR IT IS AGAINST THE RELIGION TO COMMIT SUICIDE)

<u>If there is a past attempt of suicide</u>
   1. **Did you take any steps not to be found out? (If suicide was attempted when the patient knew he/she will be at home alone and the attempt will be successful)**
   2. **When you attempted were you intoxicated?**
   3. **Did you write any suicidal note?**
   4. **Do you regret your actions of attempting suicide?**
   5. **How long did you plan before the attempt?**

6. Was it an impulsive decision?
7. Active suicidal thoughts means making planning to commit suicide
8. Passive death wishes—For example :---Wishing a car runs them over as the patient has no guts to perform an attempt.

SAD PERSON SCALE

Sex

Age

Depression

      Past history of depression

Previous attempt of suicide

Ethanol use

Rational thinking----- loss (psychosis/ excessive guilt)

Social support

Organized plan

No spouse

Questions to ask to elicit symptoms of a manic episode

PLEASE MAKE SURE THAT THE SYMPTOMS OCCUR IN THE SAME PERIOD AS THE ELEVATED/ IRRITABLE/EXPANSIVE MOOD
- **Mania occurs in an episodic manner**
- **Untreated mania usually lasts around 2 or 3 months**
- **You need to make out if this is different from premorbid self of the patient. For example is the patient normally a quiet or introverted individual?**
- **Is this how he or she usually behaves or is this a change in the behavior.**

1) **Decreased need for sleep**
   Did you ever notice that after just 2 or 3 hours of sleep you feel refreshed?
   How many hours do you usually need to sleep?
2) **Inflated self- esteem (grandiosity/ boastfulness)**
   Do you feel you can do things better than other people?
3) **Talkativeness**
   Has anyone said that you are more talkative than normal?
   Do you feel that you are more talkative?
4) **Goal directed activity**
   Do you have many plans in life?
   Do you feel that you have many/racing thoughts?
5) **Excessive involvement in pleasurable activity**
   Have you been spending more money than normal?
   Have you been throwing parties excessively (different from the usual self)?
   Have you been doing charity/ helping others more than normal?
   Have you been staying in hotels lately?
   Using substances more than usual?
   (use your judgement)
   Have you been driving faster than normal?
6) **Easily distractible?**
   Do you start a job/ work not finish it and move on to another?
   Eg arranging cupboard. Take out contents of the cupboard put it on the floor . Just leave it there for days.
   This will manifest as poor functioning as the patient cannot complete the tasks as he was distracted.
7) **Flight of ideas**
   When you are speaking to the patient you will notice that the patient jumps from one topic to another

Questions to ask to elicit psychosis

AS A PRINCIPLE ALWAYS ASK OPEN ENDED QUESTIONS AT THE BEGINNING

Hallucinations

Do you see or hear things that others cannot see or hear?

Do the voices come from outside you head?

Can you tell me from which direction the voices come from?

Do you feel afraid when you hear the voices?

Can you see the person who is talking?

Is it someone you know?

What are they saying?

Do you feel like obeying?

Can you ignore the voices?

Delusion of persecution

Do you feel any one wants to harm you?

Is someone spying on you?

Does anyone follow you?

Can you see these people?

Why would they want to do that?

How do you know this is the reason?

How long has this been going on for?

How do you cope with this problem?

Does this problem affect you?

Schneiderian first rank symptoms –this is important as 80% of the schizophrenic patients have this at some part of their illness

- Thought insertion---feel like external agency can insert thoughts into the patient's head
- Thought withdrawal-----feel like external agency can remove thoughts from the patient's head
  Do you feel someone can insert, extract or remove thoughts from your mind?
- Thought broadcast---patient feels like everyone around him knows what the patient is thinking
  Do you feel your thoughts are being broadcasted to those around you?
  Do you feel others know what you are thinking?
  How is this possible?
- Delusions of control—someone can control the patient's movements
- Do you feel others can control your actions?
  If so how is this possible that they can control it?
- Delusional perception—perception is normal but abnormal meaning is attached.
  Do you have special meaning attached to numbers?
  Do certain objects have a special significance for you?
- Third person hallucination---2 people talking about the person
  Do you hear two people discussing about you?
- Commentary hallucinations---a voice commenting on the patient
  (Do you hear someone commenting on your actions)
- Echo de la pense---hearing one's thoughts are being spoken aloud.
  (Do you hear your thoughts being spoken out aloud as though it is coming from outside your head?)

DELUSIONS MUST BE CHALLENGED

STUDENT TO SAY " IF I TOLD YOU THST IS NOT POSSIBLE WOULD YOU BELIEVE ME?'

TO BE CONSIDERED A DELUSION, THE PATIENT MUST HOLD ON TO THE BELIEF.

THE DEFINITION OF DELUSION STATES THAT IT MUST BE FIXED BELIEF

Hence it is unshakeable.

DEFINITIONS

- **DELUSION** IS A FIXED, FIRM BELIEF THAT IS HELD DESPITE EVIDENCE TO THE CONTRARY AND IS OUT OF KEEPING WITH CULTURAL NORMS.
  (Explanation of "Evidence to the contrary": For example a patient believes he has cancer despite all his tests are normal)
  (Out of keeping with cultural norms: For example walking under the ladder is bad luck. This is an example of a cultural belief so it is not a delusion.)
- **HALLUCINATION** IS A PERCEPTION IN THE ABSENCE OF A STIMULUS.
- **ILLUSION** IS MISINTERPRETATION OF EXTERNAL STIMULI.
- **MOOD** IS THE SUSTAINED INTERNAL EMOTIONAL STATE
- **AFFECT** IS THE EXTERNAL EXPRESSION OF EMOTION

Printed in the United States
by Baker & Taylor Publisher Services